everything is going to be okay, some days will be harder than others but you will get through them, it might seem like your whole world is over, you might not see any future for yourself. i promise that one day things will be better, hold on to that and keep going. breathe.

she was beautiful
but she didn't let that define her
she was brave, fierce, strong, kind, confident,
passionate and so much more
she had so much to offer the world.
be more than people can see on the outside
break boundaries
move mountains
be your wonderful self

and let the rest fall into place.

sometimes you need to break
remember that after morning breaks,
comes the day
after you break, let that be your day
you live

something as simple as a smile
can change your day

her eyes were bright like the moon,
her smile wide as the ocean

beyond this, her heart was kind
she was kind to herself
although, she never was before
she had learned that
true happiness begins with loving yourself

but don't just dream,
take your dreams and paint the world with them,
send fireworks screaming through the sky,
light up the world with your dreams.

you spend your days stuck in a mindset of self hatred
how do you escape?
take one day at a time,
accept a compliment, it doesn't make you big headed
look in the mirror and compliment yourself,
only when you let the light in
will you be able to shine

after rain comes the sun and it creates a rainbow
in time will come your sun

and then your rainbow

the day she said to her body
'i love you'
and meant it,
was the day everything changed.
she had the power within her to accept herself
for who she is,
not what society is trying to make her become
or what her demons are forcing her to be.

you might feel like today is a bad day,
but that can change
don't decide that today is bad
before you've given it a chance

don't focus on what has been,
what could have been
or even what could be.
live every moment as it comes,
take each day minute by minute
breathe every breath as though you are breathing for the
first time
and take in the beauty of the world.

when you feel alone
look up into infinity
and in that moment,
remember that this life is yours.
you will always have yourself.
become your best friend

her mind was a storm
a raging tornado of self destruction
she was at war with herself
a constant battle
she could have given up, easily
but
she was brave
she fought her demons
she let go of the past
though it was tough,
she never gave up
until
she was at peace,
with herself

take your suffering
acknowledge it's there,
but don't let it stop you.
for you are more than that,
you are a wild horse
running free on an open plain.
let your soul feel the freedom of this world
and know,
you are not defined by what you have been through

when you feel like the walls that surround you
are caving in
and you feel like there is no way out.
let your mind escape,
you have control,
transport yourself to a place
where you feel safe and calm
stay there for a while
until you are ready to face the world.

for you, i hope that one day you will see
how special you are
how much you mean to me.
you are truly wonderful,
your presence in this sometimes grey world
immediately adds beautiful bright colours
and helps me to see how
i can make a change in myself to make people feel loved
like you do.
thank you, for being you

to be able to help others,
you must first help yourself

you build walls and shut yourself off,
it won't get you anywhere
but further into the dark,
you need to knock those walls down
and let people in,

let the sun shine down on your face,
feel it's warmth radiating throughout your body.
let the wind breeze over you
and feel it within your soul.
let the rain pour down
and feel it seep into your skin
for nothing is greater than the feeling of the natural powers
this world has to offer.

bloom, don't just grow

when you feel like giving up
look up to the sky
and think
of all the possibilities
life has to offer,
and remember
how much this world needs
you

you are more than your past,
you are greater than your struggles,
you are a shining star that
lights up the sky
on a dark night

be creative,
be free,
open your mind
and let your spirit run free

how wonderful can this life be?
as wonderful as you make it.
once you realise this,
you become unstoppable

when you miss someone,
speak to them,
they aren't really gone,
they will forever be in your heart

don't just dream of a happy life,
go out there and make it happen.
the possibilities are endless
for you to enjoy.
create a life you love

sometimes all you can do is cry,
let the rivers flow freely from your eyes
surrender yourself to the freedom.
feel your pain washing away

let the universe work its magic,
let your mind be free.
allow the world to spin
and allow the stars to shine
allow your heart to heal,
in time you will thrive

smile at somebody today,
a small gesture could make
someones day

the past is the past,
the now is the now,
the future is the future.
live every day as it comes

when you feel like the walls are caving in,
look up to the sky,
and remember how strong you are,
its okay if you don't feel strong,
just let things be

if only you could see in yourself,
what i see in you.
a light that shines so bright
in the darkness of the night

those that died by suicide,
the ones we miss daily.
please don't end up like them,
we need you in this world.

they say just be patient,
but i am already a patient,
can't they see
how long i've been waiting,
to be free

one day,
you will be at peace,
just make that peace,
on this earth

there is hope for the future,
unitl you can see that,
i will hold the hope for you

sometimes you can forget,
just how needed you are.
please never forget
how much the world would lose
without you

even on the darkest nights,
the sun still rises

hope,
hold
on
pain
ends

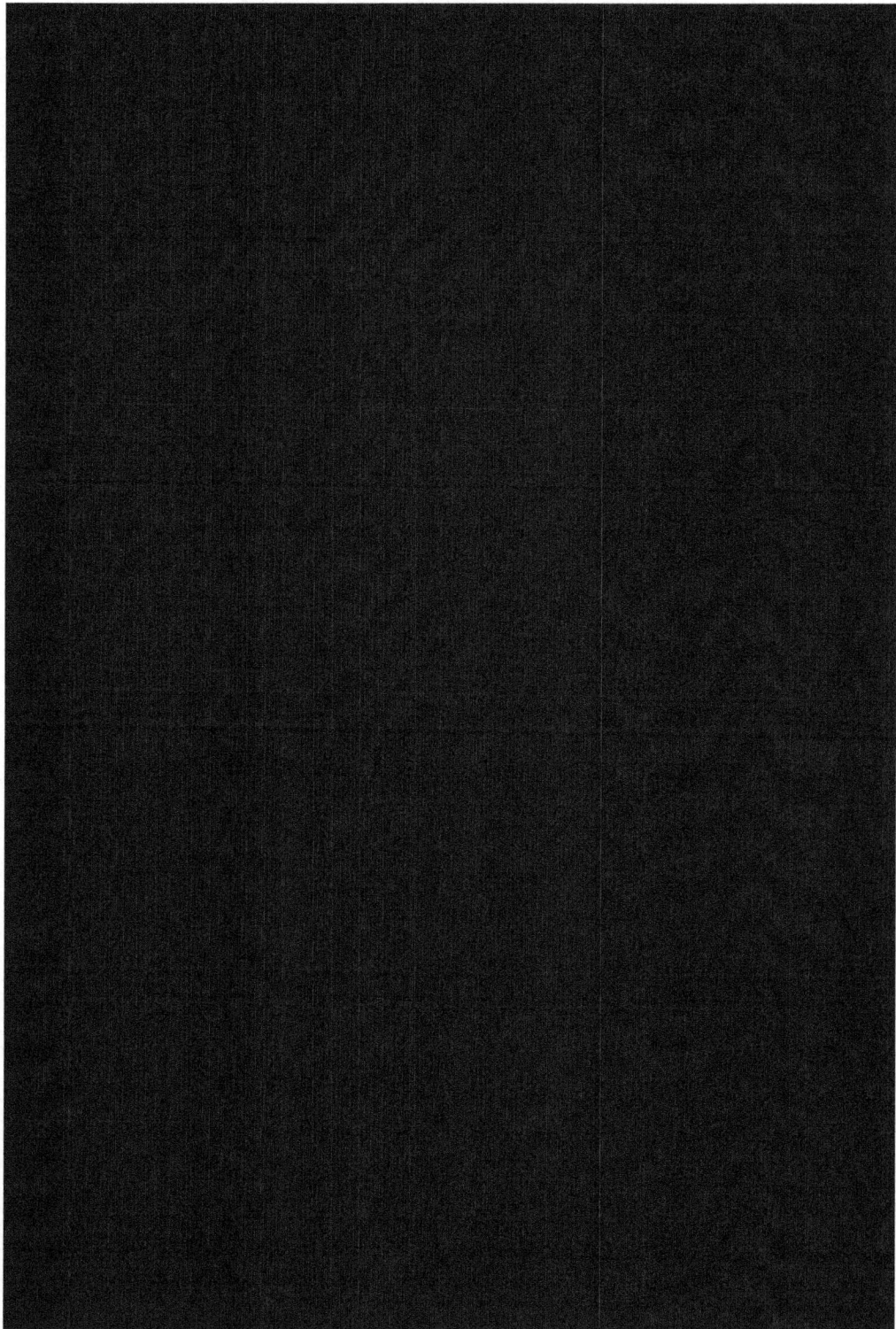

Printed in Great Britain
by Amazon